Disney's Year Book

1987

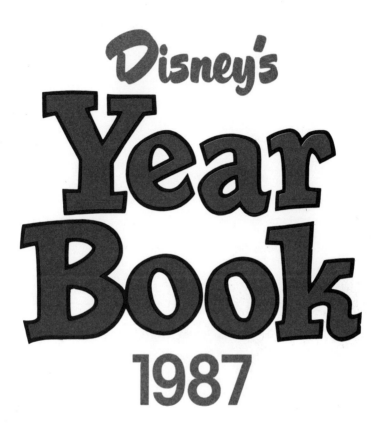

Disney's Year Book 1987

GROLIER ENTERPRISES INC.
Danbury, Connecticut

GROLIER ENTERPRISES INC.
Robert B. Clarke   *Publisher*

ISBN: 0-7172-8193-0
ISSN: 0273-1274

Illustration Credits and Acknowledgments

6—© J.P. Laffont/Sygma; 7—AP/Wide World; 8—© Christopher Mor-
ris/Black Star; 9—© 1986 Rick Friedman/ Black Star; 10—top left,
© Sygma, top right, © Culver Pictures, Inc., bottom right, © The Bettmann Archives, Inc.; 11—© Richard Berenholtz/Life Magazine; 12—
© 1986 Woods Hole Oceanographic Institution; 13—left, © 1986 Woods
Hole Oceanographic Institution, right, © 1986 Woods Hole Oceanographic Institution; 14—© The Bettmann Archives, Inc.; 15—© 1986
Woods Hole Oceanographic Institution; 28—© David Cannon/Allsport;
30—© Duomo 1986; 31—© Duomo 1986; 32-35—© Susan Copen Oken;
48-51—Courtesy of Scholastic Photography Awards, conducted by
Scholastic Magazines, Inc. and sponsored by Eastman Kodak Com-
pany; 52—Crafts by Jenny Tesar; 54—© Alex Kerstitch; 55—top,
© Chris Newbert, bottom, © Alex Kerstitch; 68-69—Caterpillars
designed and created by Michèle A. McLean; 70—© Shostal Associates; 71—© Dan Wynn; 72—left, © Bruce Coleman, Inc., right,
© Shostal Associates; 73—© Derek Fell; 74—(c) Walter Chandoha ;
75—© Design Photography International; 76—© 1984 Michelle
and Tom Grimm; 77—© Animals, Animals; 78—© Wolfgang Obst/
Obst Productions; 79—top, © Animals, Animals, bottom, © NASA;
80—© Shostal Associates; 81—© Jacques Chenet/Woodfin Camp &
Associates; 82—The Granger Collection; 83—Courtesy of Max Planck
Institut for Aeronomie.

Contents

Happy Birthday,
LADY LIBERTY!

On July 4, 1986, 40,000 skyrockets exploded in the sky above New York Harbor, and brilliant bursts of colored light slowly rained down on the Statue of Liberty.

It was the biggest fireworks display in America's history—a fitting tribute to Lady Liberty on her 100th birthday.

Thousands of spectators in the harbor and on shore were stirred by this display. Millions

"Tall ships" (below) paraded in N.Y. Harbor.

Thousands of performers took part in the huge outdoor show at Giants Stadium in New Jersey.

more watched and cheered as the scene was pictured on television. This celebration had special meaning for Americans because the Statue of Liberty is so closely tied to the meaning of America as a nation.

The Statue of Liberty was presented to America by France as a gift to commemorate the 100th birthday of the U.S., which took place in 1876. But the statue took longer to build than originally planned. It was shipped to New York in 1885 and dedicated in 1886.

The Statue of Liberty became the first landmark seen by millions of people coming to the U.S., a symbol of America's promise of a new life of freedom and opportunity.

Lady Liberty's birthday celebration lasted for four days—and it was a wonderful party! On Thursday, July 3, President Ronald Reagan pulled switches that relit the statue and its torch, which had been darkened while it was being restored and rebuilt.

On July 4, U.S. warships and sailing ships from around the world paraded in the harbor.

Two happy guests at the Statue's birthday party in N.Y. Harbor.

FIRST SIGHT OF LIBERTY

The Statue of Liberty, created by the French sculptor Frédéric Bartholdi, is 131 feet tall. It is hollow and was made in sections which were then shipped to the U.S. (above right, a model of the head on display in France.)

The Statue welcomed millions of people from foreign lands to America's shores. It was the first landmark seen by families such as this one (above) as they steamed into N.Y. Harbor. For the Statue's birthday celebration, a group of immigrants was sworn in as citizens on Ellis Island (above left).

For its birthday party, the 151-foot tall statue was repaired and restored inside and out. The new torch (right) has gold leaf covering the flames, as in the sculptor's original design.

In the evening came the giant fireworks display, along with a stirring concert.

On Saturday, the Statue was open to visitors. On shore, thousands of people enjoyed a harbor festival featuring food and entertainment. The grand and glorious celebration ended on Sunday with a huge televised show at Giant Stadium.

Happy Birthday, Lady Liberty!

EXPLORING
THE TITANIC
2½ MILES UNDER THE SEA

Minisub Alvin *and mother ship* Atlantis II *at the site of the sunken* Titanic *in the North Atlantic.*

Just before midnight on April 14, 1912, the giant luxury liner *Titanic* struck an iceberg in the northern Atlantic. Within three hours, the great ship sank beneath the waves.

The *Titanic* was the largest ship built up to that time, and this was her first voyage. Only about 700 of some 2,200 people on board were saved because there were not enough lifeboats to take everyone off. The ship was supposed to be "unsinkable." It had a double hull and its builders were sure that if one hull was pierced, the second hull would keep the ship afloat.

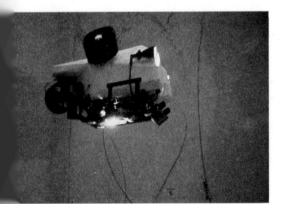

Dr. Robert Ballard (right) led the Titanic *expedition, which used robot Jason Jr. (left) to explore the ship.*

An artist's version shows the Titanic *going down.*

It seemed that the mystery of how the *Titanic* sank would never be solved. Then, in 1985, the remains of the ship were found off the coast of Newfoundland, lying on the ocean floor 2½ miles down.

In 1986, a U.S. expedition set out to explore the wreck. The explorers used a special minisub, *Alvin,* designed to withstand the great water pressure at such depths. When *Alvin* got close to the wreck, it sent out a robot, Jason Jr. (JJ) that entered the ship and took photos inside. JJ's photos showed that the ship's crystal chandeliers and many other decorations were still intact more than 70 years after the disaster.

The explorers saw that the ship had broken in two before it reached the bottom. They found no hole in the hull from the collision with the iceberg. They now believe that when the ship hit the iceberg, the steel plates of the two hulls were forced apart. Water then poured in, sinking the "unsinkable" ship.

One of many photographs taken by the robot Jason Jr. as it explored the Titanic *shows a porthole on the sunken luxury liner.*

Captain Hook's Flying Scheme

Captain Hook paced the deck of his pirate ship. "I must find a way to get rid of Peter Pan. I must take over Never Land," he muttered.

Hook raised his spyglass and caught a glimpse of Peter Pan flying with his friends, Wendy and John and Michael.

"If only I could fly!" grumbled Captain Hook. "I'd make my ship and crew fly. And I'd chase Peter Pan out of Never Land!"

Suddenly Captain Hook had an idea. "Smee, front and center!" he cried. "All hands on deck!" Then Hook told his men how they would take over Never Land.

The crew got busy. Some got needles and
thread. Some looked for green felt and glue.
Some found buttons. And Captain Hook sat
down to write a note. It read:

My dear Miss Bell
I would like to meet
you. Please fly over
Pirate's Cove. I will
be waiting.
Your Secret Admirer

Tinker Bell jingled merrily when she read
the note. Someone wanted to meet her. Who
could it be?

Leaving the note behind, Tink darted off to
Pirates Cove. She flew across it three times,
but she saw no secret admirer. She did see
the pirate ship. Surely her admirer wasn't a
pirate! Then she glanced down, and to her

surprise, she saw
Peter Pan tied to the
mast of the pirate ship.

Tinker Bell flew to
the rescue. She
landed on Peter's
shoulder. But it wasn't
Peter Pan!

It was a dummy made of cloth and green felt!
Its button eyes stared.

Tinker Bell tried to take off again—but her
feet were stuck. The dummy's shoulder was
covered with sticky glue!

"Good day, Miss Bell,"
said Captain Hook.
"We're so glad you could
join us." The pirates
all laughed.

"I have a small
favor to ask,"
Hook said.
"Sprinkle my crew
and ship with
pixie dust so

we can fly." Tinker Bell shook her head furiously.

Captain Hook shut Tinker Bell up in a ship's lantern. "There you'll stay until you've changed your mind!" he sneered.

Back at Hangman's Tree, Peter Pan was holding an emergency meeting with Wendy, John, Michael and the Lost Boys.

"Tinker Bell is missing," he began. "Wendy found this note." And Peter read the note aloud.

"I'll bet Captain Hook is behind this," said Peter. "I'm going to fly out to the pirate ship."

"Let us go with you," said John.

"No!" said Peter. "Without Tinker Bell, you can't fly with me. You'd have to go in a boat. The pirates would see us."

"But, Peter!" said Wendy. "If you do find Tinker Bell, you can't fight a ship full of pirates alone. You'll need our help."

Peter thought for a minute. "I have just the thing," he said, "something I've been saving for a long time."

Peter opened a small cupboard. He took
out two dusty jars. One was marked "Fairy
Dust," the other "Troll Dust."

"Now watch this," he said. He sprinkled
some fairy dust on John. He disappeared. A
few minutes later he blinked back into view.

"What happened?" asked Wendy.

Peter explained. "Fairy dust makes you
disappear. We can use it to get to the pirate

ship without
being seen."

"What about the troll
dust?" asked John.

"It can be dangerous
stuff," Peter warned.
"It can turn you to

stone and it takes a
long time to wear off.
But we'll take it
along, just in case."

Meanwhile, Captain Hook
had persuaded Tinker
Bell to sprinkle pixie dust
on his crew by threatening
to hurt Peter Pan.

"Smee! Front and center!" Hook ordered.

Tinker Bell sprinkled the first mate with pixie dust. Hook threw Smee overboard to see if he would fly. There was a big splash. The pirates pulled Smee out of the water.

"Why didn't he fly?" cried Captain Hook. Then he remembered.

"Try again," he ordered Smee. "This time think happy thoughts. If you think happy thoughts, the pixie dust will work."

Smee tried hard to think a happy thought as Tinker Bell kept sprinkling. But his feet stayed on the deck.

Suddenly an umbrella hit the pirate captain over the head. John popped into sight, holding on to the handle.

Then Peter Pan appeared. He sliced the big feather off Captain Hook's hat.

The fight was on. Boys began appearing all over the deck. John bashed a pirate with his umbrella. Michael hit another with his teddy bear.

While the battle raged, Wendy freed Tinker Bell and handed her the bottle of troll dust. The little pixie jingled happily and flew around the ship, spreading a cloud of troll dust over everyone.

Wendy looked on in horror. "You've sprinkled everyone!" she gasped. "We'll all turn to stone!"

Then she heard Peter's laugh. "It's all right, Wendy," he explained. "Troll dust only works when you are thinking wicked thoughts. The only ones who turned to stone were the pirates."

Wendy sighed in relief. Then Tinker Bell sprinkled them with pixie dust and they all flew back to Hangman's Tree.

And what happened to Captain Hook and his crew? Well, the last we knew, he was thinking up another plan to take over Never Land. Do you think he'll ever succeed?

Soccer's Pint-Sized
New Superstar

*Small but powerful Maradonna is the newest
star of soccer, the world's most popular sport.*

His nickname is *Dieguito*, "little Diego" in Spanish, because he's just 5'5" tall and weighs 152 pounds. But to many soccer fans, Diego Armando Maradona of Argentina is the best soccer player in the world.

And when he led the Argentinian team to victory in the 1986 World Cup tournament in Mexico, he got a new nickname—*El Rey*, "The King."

The World Cup is the "World Series" of soccer. Held every four years, it's so popular

that this year nine billion fans in 152 countries watched the games on television.

In the World Cup's exciting final match, Argentina beat West Germany by the score of 3-2.

Maradonna battling hard in the World Cup.

Delighted Maradonna holds the World Cup after Argentina beat West Germany in the final.

Maradona was clearly the outstanding player in the tournament. As a mid-fielder, his main job was to set up plays so that his teammates could score. But Maradona scored four goals himself. Strong and fast, he charged through opposing defenders with dazzling skill to put the ball in the net from close range.

As the Argentinian coach said after his team won, Maradona "has to be the best . . . He is the World Cup."

HAVE YOU HUGGED
YOUR PIG TODAY?

Pigs are in! Once they were just dirty old barnyard beasts. Now they're turning up on T-shirts and greeting cards and starring in movies and cartoons. Now people are wearing plastic pig snouts and pig-eared hats and decorating the walls of their homes with pig paintings and pig posters.

And those who love pigs best are keeping pigs as pets. Pig owners are proud to say that pigs are not lazy, fat, dirty animals, good only for eating. On the contrary, they're cute, cuddly, clean pets who can bring pounds of pleasure into anyone's life.

Lovable pigs are becoming popular pets.

Next best thing to being a pig is looking like one.

Pig lovers want people to know that a lot of lies have been told about pigs. For example, the idea that a sweaty person "sweats like a pig." Actually, pigs hardly sweat at all because they have very few sweat glands. To cool off in hot weather, pigs have to lie in something wet. Pigs would rather lie in nice clean water than in the mud of a pigsty. But they usually can only find mud.

Another lie is that pigs overeat and are messy eaters. That's not true. Pigs do like all sorts of food, and pet pigs have been known to eat anything from chocolate chip cookies to lobster.

In fact, pigs are among the most intelligent of all domestic animals. They can be trained to do all sorts of things—pull wagons, chew bubble gum, and even perform "dog tricks" like sitting, lying down, and rolling over. Pigs can also be taught to swim, and one became a heroine when she saved a boy from drowning in a lake.

In short, pigs are the greatest! Pigs are in! Have you hugged *your* pig today?

Who says pigs can't do anything but eat?

THE KIDDIN' KITTENS

"Marie! Hide!" whispered Berlioz to his sister. Both Aristokittens ducked behind the grand piano's heavy legs. Then they began crying pitifully.

O'Malley, the alley cat, and Toulouse, the other Aristokitten, rushed into the room. The meows sounded as if they were coming from inside the piano.

"Those poor kittens!" panted O'Malley. "I've got to get them out!" He hooked his claws under the heavy piano top. Then he lifted it a few inches. "Quick!" he called to Toulouse. "Get me something to prop the lid open!"

Then he heard giggling.

O'Malley looked under the lid. No kittens. Suddenly the room was filled with kittenish giggles.

"Hee-hee! You were so funny!" Berlioz gasped. He and Marie came out from their hiding place.

"We fooled you, didn't we?" added Marie.

The piano lid fell with a loud *bang!* The kittens stopped laughing. "Toulouse, you told me your brother and sister were trapped in the piano," said O'Malley. "That wasn't very nice!"

Berlioz giggled. "It was just a joke."

"I don't think much of your jokes," said O'Malley. And he stalked out.

A little while later Duchess and O'Malley were playing a game of chess. Berlioz ran in. "Mama!" he cried. "Toulouse and Marie are in trouble! A big black dog has them cornered!"

"O'Malley! You must rescue them!" cried Duchess.

O'Malley gave Berlioz a funny look, but he said, "Let's go, kid."

Berlioz led O'Malley out to the alley. Sure enough, a large black dog crouched there. He was making crunching noises.

O'Malley leaped, spitting and snarling, on the dog's tail.

The hound squealed in pain and shook O'Malley off. He went howling down the alley, leaving behind a big bone.

Then O'Malley heard giggles. Toulouse, Marie and Berlioz were laughing so hard they couldn't stand up.

"Oh, Monsieur O'Malley, you were so funny!"

"Another joke!" O'Malley said. He was so angry he couldn't even speak. He stalked away.

Later that afternoon, O'Malley and Duchess were talking. "They're just going through a stage, O'Malley," said Duchess.

"Stage or not, Duchess, it has to stop. This new game they're playing is too mean."

"You're right, of course," Duchess began.

Suddenly Roquefort the
mouse hurried into the room.
"Come quick!" he squeaked.
"Marie has fallen into the
well!"

"Wait a minute,"
O'Malley said. "Where
are her brothers?"
He turned to Roquefort.

"They've put you up to this, haven't they?"

"Put me up . . . But Monsieur, they are in
the garden, too!"

"Come on, Roquefort. Those kittens have been driving me crazy all day. You just tell them it won't work this time."

Then Duchess spoke. "I don't think our friend Roquefort would have anything to do with tricking us."

"Well, all right," O'Malley said. "Let's go. But those kittens better not be fooling again."

When they got to the garden they saw that Roquefort had been telling the truth. Berlioz and Toulouse had lowered the well bucket to their sister. But they weren't strong enough to pull her out. The rope was beginning to fray.

O'Malley told Roquefort to get Frou-Frou, Madame's carriage horse. Soon Frou-Frou clattered into the garden.

"Take hold of the rope, Frou-Frou," said O'Malley.

"You're the only one strong enough to pull
up the bucket. But pull back slowly. We don't
want that old rope to break."

Carefully Frou-Frou grasped the rope in
her teeth. Slowly she backed up, pulling
Marie and the bucket up out of the well.

Just in time, O'Malley grabbed Marie by
the scruff of the neck. At that moment, the
rope broke.

The bucket splashed back down
into the well.

Marie looked shyly at O'Malley. "How can I
ever thank you?" she said. "Especially after
those tricks we played on you."

"I'm just glad you're
safe." he answered.
Then he looked at all
three Aristokittens.
"I hope you have
learned your lesson,"
he added.

"Of course," Berlioz said. "Next time we want to fool you, we must get Monsieur Roquefort to help."

O'Malley growled at the kittens.

"No, no!" Berlioz was quick to say. "We have learned. I was only fooling."

STRIPES
AND
SPOTS

When you look at a giraffe, do you see the very special pattern of spots it wears? The photographer does, and snaps a photograph that shows the beauty of this image.

The photographer sees what we may miss in the world—and produces photographs that turn everyday sights into works of art.

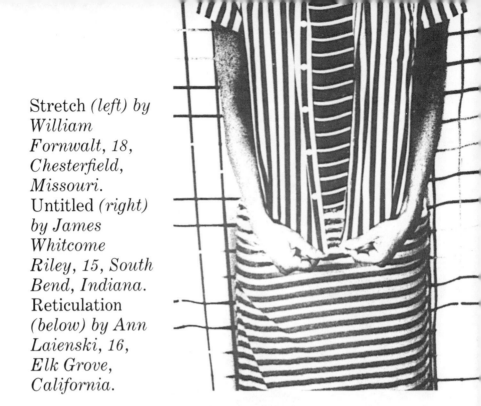

Stretch *(left)* by William Fornwalt, 18, Chesterfield, Missouri. Untitled *(right)* by James Whitcome Riley, 15, South Bend, Indiana. Reticulation *(below)* by Ann Laienski, 16, Elk Grove, California.

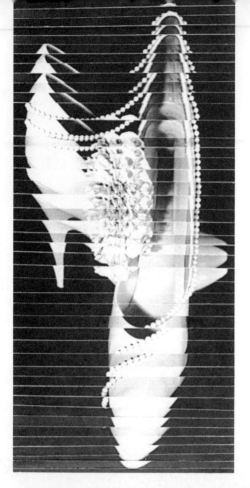

String Along *(left) by
Lisa McDonald, 17,
Chesterfield,
Missouri.* Balloonrise
*(below) by Eric Thun,
17, Dewitt, New York.*
Studying *(right) by
Lurline Tau'a, 14,
Waianae, Hawaii.*

The photographs on these pages were among the winners in the 1986 Scholastic/Kodak Photo Award Program. This program is open to students in junior and senior high schools in the United States and Canada. The winners receive scholarships and other awards.

THE WRITE STUFF

Dear Mother,
 We are out of ice cream. Please buy some today.
  Love xxx
   Sally

Dear Sally,
 You have had enough ice cream this week.
  Love xxx
   Mother

Nothing is handier to have around the house than a note pad, and this one is really fun to make.

What You'll Need

Food strainer, pink cloth, yarn, felt, pad, pencil, tape and glue, needle and thread

What to Do

1. Use a small strainer for the doll's head. Cover the mesh with pink cloth—but don't cover the hook at the top of the strainer. Sew the cloth tight in back.
2. Make the doll's hair from yarn and glue it to the face.
3. Make the doll's eyes, nose, and mouth by cutting out pieces of felt—red for the mouth, of course. Glue the felt to the cloth. Then make a felt bow for the doll's neck.
4. Tape the note pad to the strainer handle. Then tape two loops of felt to the back of the pad to hold a pencil.
5. Hang the strainer by its hook.

Now you're ready to write your first message!

Sea Colors

The creatures and landscapes that are
found beneath tropical seas present a riot of
dazzling colors.

One reason that sea creatures have such
brilliant hues is to protect them from their
enemies. Against the background of colored
reefs and plants, they blend in and become
invisible to animals hunting them.

The bright colors of a sea creature may also
be a warning to its enemies that it is

The angelfish (left), the pipefish (above), and the psychedelic dragonet (below) brighten tropic seas.

poisonous. An octopus that gets stung by a poisonous red fish will remember that fish's color and stay away from it.

The special colors of different species also allow males and females of the species to find each other at mating time, when the reef is crowded with hundreds of different kinds of sea animals.

THE GREEDY TROLLS

Once upon a time there was a sunny, peaceful valley with a big tree in the middle of it.

The big tree was home to all sorts of birds and squirrels. People came to the valley from miles around to picnic and play with their friends.

Jonathan and his sister, Miriam, went there whenever they could.

Jonathan would climb in the tree with the other boys, and Miriam would pay hide-and-seek with the other girls. Sometimes all the boys and girls together would play a game of tag around the tree.

One day a family of
trolls came to the
valley. They stopped
at the big tree.

"This looks like a
good place to dig a
home," grunted
the papa troll.

"Oh, yes!" said the mama troll, "It's much
too nice to leave it alone."

The troll family started digging their home
under the big tree. They dug day and night.
It wasn't very long before the tree started to
die.

"Ah! This is perfect," laughed the papa
troll. "There's nothing better than a home
under the roots of a dying tree."

The next day
Jonathan and Miriam
came to the valley for
a picnic. Suddenly, the
trolls popped out and
grabbed all their picnic
food.

"Hey! Wait a minute! Why did you take our food?" yelled Jonathan.

"Because taking things is what trolls do best," laughed the little boy troll.

"We work for the ogre," snarled the papa troll. "He's going to pay us for all the food we can take."

Then the troll family scurried back home.

"Well, next time we'd better picnic in the middle of the field," said Miriam. And she

slammed the lid
shut on their empty
picnic basket.

The next day,
Jonathan and Miriam
spread their picnic
blanket far away
from the big tree. But
the trolls burrowed
under the

ground. They popped
up next to the picnic
blanket and grabbed
everything they could.

"Next time we come
here, we'd better leave
our food at home," said
Miriam. "Otherwise the
trolls will just take it."
The next day Jonathan
and Miriam spread

their picnic blanket in another open field. Sure enough, the trolls popped up to grab all the food. They were surprised to find that there was no food to grab.

"Silly trolls!" laughed Miriam. "How does it feel to have nothing to grab?"

Jonathan and Miriam picked up their picnic blanket and ran home, laughing all the way.

"Well," snorted the papa troll, "we'll just have to find something else to take. Our boss, the ogre, will be coming soon. We must show

him we're doing
a good job."

So the trolls took all
the fruit from the
trees in the valley and
hid it in their dark
home. Then they
took all the berries
from the berry bushes
in the valley. And
then they

took all the nuts from the nut trees. They
even took the eggs from the birds' nests.

When the trolls had taken everything, the
birds and squirrels moved away from the
valley. There was nothing left to eat.

Finally, the ogre arrived. He pushed his

way right past the
trolls to the fruit,
nuts and berries.

"Give me that and
that and those and that
and these and this and
that and those!" he

snorted. He
grabbed everything
he could, which
was everything the
trolls had.

Then he threw
each of the trolls a
rotten peach.

"You're all fired!
he said. And he
disappeared from view.

"Well, how do you like that?" grumbled the papa troll.

"He didn't even give us two weeks' notice," said the mama troll.

"These peaches are too rotten to eat," complained the little boy troll.

"I'm hungry!" cried the little girl troll.

Squatting at the base of the big tree, the trolls all started crying.

Jonathan and Miriam came to the valley to see what had happened. They brought a basket of food with them, just in case.

As soon as they set out their picnic blanket and basket, the trolls spotted them.

"Uh-oh, Jonathan—here they come again," sighed Miriam.

But this time the trolls didn't take anything. They just sat down near Jonathan and Miriam and watched.

"Let's offer them something," said Miriam.

Jonathan pulled out
a nice, ripe peach. He
handed it to the mama troll. But the mama
troll didn't eat it. Instead, she gave it to the
little boy troll.

The little boy troll passed the peach to the
little girl troll. "You're the one who's
hungry," he said.

Jonathan and Miriam passed out more food.

"This is fun! I don't mind sharing my food with you trolls when you don't grab it," said Miriam.

"We like it this way, too," admitted the papa troll. "We really didn't like working for that ogre."

"The pay was lousy, too," snorted the mama troll, biting into a juicy peach.

"Well," said Jonathan, "this is a better way to make friends, I think."

Soon the fruit, nuts and berries were
growing on the trees again. Then the birds
and squirrels came back to the valley.

Soon Jonathan and Miriam and all their
friends were playing and picnicking with the
troll family.

The trolls were especially good at playing
hide-and-seek.

MAKE FRIENDS WITH A
CATERPILLAR

Everyone needs a pal, and one of these
cute and creepy critters can be yours.

You can make your caterpillar from knee-
socks (patterned ones work best). Do the
caterpillar's head first by stuffing the toe of

the sock with cotton or other soft material.
Then stuff the other sections, tying yarn
around each one.

Use pipe cleaners and pompons for the
antennae and legs. Make the eyes from felt or
plastic and add false eyelashes.

Now, say "hello" to your caterpillar!

Your Nose Knows

Some things have a very special smell—like a Christmas tree or a cake baking in the oven.

But how do you recognize that smell when you smell it? Your nose does it. Your nose smells chemicals—they're called odor molecules—that are sent out by whatever it is you are smelling.

The pleasant aroma of flowers (above) and chocolate (right) makes most people feel happy.

The odor molecules rise through the nostrils to the back of the nose. Nerve cells in the lining of the nose then send signals about the smell to a part of the brain that is just behind the eyes. This part is called the olfactory bulb. (Olfactory means relating to the sense of smell.)

From the olfactory bulb, the signals go deeper into the brain. The brain then tells you what you are smelling.

Scientists know this much about the sense of smell, but they still don't know exactly how the brain tells one smell from another.

The sense of smell and the sense of taste work together. Many of the flavors you "taste" in a food are really smells. When you eat chocolate, for example, you know it's chocolate because it releases odor molecules that enter your nose.

Scientists have discovered that we would not be able to "taste" many foods if our sense of smell was not working.

The sense of smell is also related to other things that our brains control, such as memory and emotion.

The "taste" of many foods such as watermelon and pizza comes from their very special aromas.

People usually remember smells, such as that of apples, longer than they do sights and sounds.

People remember smells longer and better than they remember things they see or hear. If you smell an aroma you've smelled before, you'll probably remember where and how you smelled it.

If smelling it before was an unpleasant experience, you'll be reminded of it. If the experience was pleasant, such as smelling a flower on a spring day, you'll be reminded of that—and you'll feel good again.

Why Animals
Do What They Do

*Cats and dogs do many things that their wild
ancestors do. But as pets, they learn how to
behave by living in human households.*

When you come home, your dog runs to greet you. When you go out, it may howl for hours. But your cat doesn't seem to care very much whether you're home or not.

What makes cats and dogs act the way they do? The answer lies in their nature. Cats and dogs are descended from wild animals. Living with people has changed them in many ways, but they still have some of the same instincts their wild relatives have.

In the wild, wolves and dogs hunt in packs. Each wolf pack has a leader.

For a dog, the human family takes the place of the pack. That's why a dog will bark and feel insecure when it's left alone. The dog will also respond to one person in the family as the leader. And a dog will always look up to people and hope for their approval, because it feels the need to belong to a pack.

Cats, on the other hand, usually hunt alone in the wild. For this reason, a domestic cat isn't bothered by the absence of people. This is also why cats seem independent. They do not feel the need to win approval from their human families.

Animals do what they do for very special reasons of their own. An animal may do something that seems similar to what a human does. But the animal's action may

Both cats and dogs love to play. In the wild, they teach themselves to hunt by playing games.

African elephants bathe in mud for a reason.

have a totally different meaning. Scientists
have discovered many examples of this.

Why Elephants Take Mud Baths: An
African elephant loves to roll around in the
mud. It may look like the elephant is playing,
but actually the elephant is using the mud to
cool off on a hot day and to soothe its itching
hide. The mud also serves as a coating
that protects the elephant from insect bites.

Racoons seem to be washing whatever they find in the water. Actually, they are looking for snails, mussels, and other water creatures to eat.

Why Ducklings Follow Their Mother:

Ducklings and other ground birds can stand up and run soon after they are hatched. The first thing they do is to follow something that is moving. Usually this is their mother. But if for some reason their mother is not around, they will follow anything that moves—a dog or a person, for example.

Ducklings may not always follow their mother.

Whatever they follow for a short time, they become attached to, and then they won't follow anything else.

This is also true of animals such as cows and sheep. Remember Mary's lamb in the nursery rhyme? "Wherever Mary went, the lamb was sure to go."

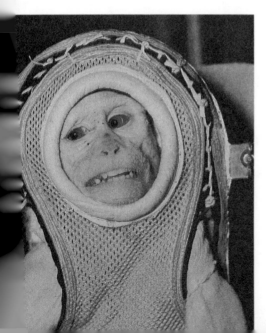

A chimpanzee that seems to be grinning, like this one being used for research on a space flight, is actually showing fear, not happiness.

A Special Visitor from Space

It only appears every 75 to 77 years. But when Halley's comet comes to visit, as it did in 1986, the occasion is special.

During the comet's previous visit in 1910, people became quite frightened. They thought they might be poisoned by gases

Halley's comet blazing through space in 1986.

from the comet's tail and they swallowed "comet pills" and wore gas masks to protect themselves.

In 1986, people welcomed the chance to see Halley's comet—and scientists set up many projects to study it. Astronomers on Earth looked at the comet through powerful telescopes, and scientists launched five unmanned spacecraft to study and photograph it in space.

These scientific studies provided more information about Halley's comet than was learned in all the centuries before 1986.

Hats, T-shirts and numerous other items were marketed to commemorate 1986 visit of the comet.

Edmund Halley (left) lived from 1656 to 1742. He saw the comet named after him in 1682 and predicted it would return in 1758—but did not live to see his prediction come true.

Halley's comet was first seen thousands of years ago. Each time it came back, people thought it was a new comet. They had no idea *why* a comet appeared, so they believed that the coming of a comet meant a terrible event would soon occur.

An English astronomer, Edmund Halley, was the first person to realize that comets reappear because they travel in an orbit through space.

A comet's head or nucleus is composed mainly of ice and frozen gases. The nucleus looks round. But scientists in 1986 discovered

This color-enhanced photo of the comet shows its nucleus, which is the dark mass at the upper left.

that it is actually shaped like a potato or peanut. When a comet approaches the sun, some of its nucleus melts and forms a cloud, called the coma, around the nucleus. The comet's tail is formed when solar winds push some of the coma away from the sun. A comet doesn't send off light. It is visible mainly because it reflects the sun's light.

In 1986, people on Earth were delighted to see Halley's comet streak across the sky. And for those who missed it, there's always 2071, the year it will come to visit again.

A Pup Of
A Different Color

Scamp burst out of the doghouse as fast as his legs would carry him. His brother and sisters raced after him.

Scamp raced straight for the trash cans, which were full of bright wrapping paper and ribbons. "Maybe there's some birthday cake left!" he cried.

"I don't know if we should do this, Scamp," argued Scooter. But Scamp was tugging at a piece of ribbon. Sure enough, the trash can toppled over with a crash and a clatter.

Jim Dear rushed outside and found Scamp sitting in a pile of trash. A birthday bow hung around his neck.

"You sure have a nose for trouble," Jim Dear exclaimed. "See if you can keep out of mischief for the rest of the day. All right?"

"You'd better be careful," said Ruffy.

"I will," the mischievous pup promised. And then he let out a gasp. "Oh, look!"

A long ladder was leaning on the house.

"It's a burglar!" exclaimed Scamp. "Let's get him!" Fluffy stopped him.

"Wait a minute," she told him. "It's broad daylight. Mother's inside and Father's around here somewhere. If it's a burglar, they'll stop him."

Soon a man wearing overalls came walking around the house. In one hand was a large brush. In the other was a bucket of paint.

"He doesn't look like a burglar," said Ruffy.

But Scamp wasn't sure. "I think I'd better get closer, just to find out."

"Hold on, laddie." Scamp's neighbor, Jock the Scottie, came into the yard. "He's no burglar."

"Nope. It looks like he's here to paint the
house," said Trusty, the bloodhound.

"Trusty's right, Scamp."

Scamp turned around and saw his mother,
Lady. "I think you pups should stay as far
away from that painter as possible. And
Scamp, you've been in enough trouble for one
day."

Fluffy and Ruffy went off to chase a
butterfly. Scamp hid behind a hedge to watch
the painter.

"Care to join me for a walk to the park?"

Scamp turned around. His father, Tramp, was standing behind him.

"Gee, thanks, Pop. But I'm supposed to be good today. Jim Dear says I have a nose for trouble."

"Suit yourself," Tramp replied. "Sounds pretty dull to me."

Finally the painter packed up his brushes

and went home. He left his long ladder leaning up against the house and several cans of paint.

That night the lights in the house were dark. Everyone in the family was fast asleep, except for Scamp. As soon as the coast was clear, he dashed toward the house.

A full moon was shining down on the yard like a bright spotlight. "Oh, boy!" thought the pup. "Now I'll see what that painter was really doing."

As he sniffed away at the first paint can, the lid fell off. Scamp saw that the paint was yellow—just like the new paint on the house.

Suddenly, he heard footsteps.
Scamp scurried behind the nearest bush.

In the moonlight he saw a man, but it
wasn't Jim Dear. It wasn't the painter,
either. The man was dressed all in black and
he wore a black mask. He began to climb up
the ladder. The fur on Scamp's back stood
straight up.

"This isn't right!" he said to himself. He
burst out of the bushes, barking as loudly as
he could.

A light went on in the house and the man
slid down the ladder. Scamp nipped at his

heels and made the man step right into a can of paint. Scamp felt paint splash all over him. But the strange man was gone!

By the time Scamp could see through the yellow paint, both Jim Dear and Darling were looking down at him. Neither of them looked very happy.

"Now I have to clean you up!" Jim cried to Scamp. "Then you'll have to be punished!"

By the time Jim Dear had scrubbed all of the yellow paint off Scamp, the morning sunlight was peeking through the big trees.

Jim put Scamp on a rope and marched him outside, past the ladder and the puddle of spilled paint.

Suddenly Scamp looked down at the ground and let out a loud yelp! He stopped dead in his tracks.

"What is wrong with you?" asked Jim Dear. Then he saw exactly what Scamp saw. Bright yellow footprints led from the spilled

paint can across the yard and
into the street.

"This is a matter for the
police!" cried Jim.

Just then, Tramp strolled
into the yard. "What's
up, pup?" he asked.

Scamp gulped hard. "I think Jim Dear is
going to send me to jail!"

"What? Oh, Scamp, come on!"

"Well, I got paint all over me last night and
now he's calling the police!"

Tramp hung around until Officer Moran

arrived. Jim Dear pointed out the yellow
footprints.

"Someone must have tried to break in here
last night," Jim Dear explained to the police
officer. "And Scamp scared him away!"

Officer Moran hurried off, following the
footprints.

"What I think you need, Scamp . . ." began
Jim Dear. Scamp closed his eyes, waiting to
hear his punishment. "What you need is a
nice, big breakfast!"

It wasn't long before Officer Moran came
back with good news. He had followed the

bright yellow footprints to a shack several
blocks away, where he found the would-be
burglar hiding.

"He's in jail now," announced Officer
Moran. "But we would never have found him
if this fellow hadn't been on guard!" He bent
down and gave Scamp a pat.

"That's what I always say—Scamp here
has a nose for trouble!" Jim Dear bragged.